Santa Muerte Prayer Magick

Affordable Santa Muerte Magick

You Can Do Anywhere

By: Arnold Bustillo

SantaMuerteMagick.com

Table of Contents

Introduction

As the owner of a website dedicated to the practice of Santa Muerte magick (SantaMuerteMagick.com), I get a lot of emails from folks wondering if they can practice Santa Muerte magick even if they don't have all the right tools. Typically they wonder what to do if they can't erect a Santa Muerte altar, or how to go about their magick if they can't get their hands on a specific herb or oil.

For starters, it is important to say that the devotion to Santa Muerte and the practice of Santa Muerte magick are not rooted in any specific tools. The power of magick is derived from our relationship with Santa Muerte, not whether or not we can erect an altar or procure a specific herb. It is our very mortality which makes the magick of Santa Muerte available to us all. The fact that we will all one day die means that none of us are forsaken by Santa Muerte. Whether we choose to accept it or not, she is in fact coming for us, and we only get closer to her embrace with every passing day.

The magickal recipes I share on my website are generally intended to be performed at or near a Santa Muerte altar. They typically involve the use of herbs, oils, and candles, along with the recitation of specific prayers, but these recipes are by no means hard and fast requirements. There is, after all, more than one way to skin a cat. The magickal rituals and formulas I share on my site are written for the best case scenario, when you have access to an area where the ritual can be performed and when you can easily procure all the ritual tools described.

While the power of Santa Muerte magick comes from our relationship with the folk saint, the power of magick in general comes from intent. From the most complicated of magickal rituals to the most basic of magickal charms, it is the intent of the magickian which is the lowest common denominator shared across all traditions of magick. Even some of the most secular, down to Earth people, recognize the great power which comes from identifying and fixating on the intent behind their actions. As devotees of Santa Muerte, we are able to blend our intent with our open acceptance of our relationship with Santa Muerte in order to receive miracles and blessings which can only be described as magickal.

My website was born at a time when I was living in Tijuana, Mexico, a city where devotion to Santa Muerte is visible in the streets, and one where the plethora of *botanicas* (spiritual supply shops) made it easy to find practically all the supplies I needed to create the magick I was writing about. If ever a magickal ingredient was not available in Tijuana, then I could order the item off the internet. Since I'm a huge supporter of writing magick for yourself, the spells and rituals shared on my website were written, above all, for me, based on what I had available to me and what I could afford.

As the following for my website has grown exponentially beyond what I ever could have imagined, I've come to realize that, for one reason or another, many of the spells and rituals I write about on my website are out of reach for people who wish to practice

Santa Muerte magick. I've been contacted by people living with uptight Christians who forbid open devotion to Santa Muerte, people who are unemployed / underemployed with little disposable income to spare, and even people behind bars who simply do not have free access to the tools I write about. Above all, I write this book for them, so that people of any economic status, in any circumstance, may enjoy active participation in the magick that Santa Muerte has to offer.

This being said, you do not have to be poor or desperate to use the information in this book. This book offers a great place to start for beginners who want to approach Santa Muerte slowly, for experienced devotees traveling away from their home altars, and practicing magickians who want to adapt these instructions for use on their own spiritual paths. It is my experience, however, that lazy efforts beget lazy results. If you are using the information in this book because you lack the freedom or permission to erect an altar where you are, or because you cannot afford the magick tools I describe on my website, then you are not acting out of laziness, you are simply responding to the reality of your circumstances. If, on the other hand, you are using this book because you can't be bothered to get off your ass to track down the magick tools I prescribe, or because you can't be bothered to invest the time to perform a full petition ritual, then you are just being lazy, and you should not be surprised if your lazy efforts produce little to no results.

The Altar

If the relationship to Santa Muerte is the foundation for Santa Muerte magick, then the altar is a representation of that relationship. However, just as a wedding ring is a representation of a marriage, the absence of a wedding ring does not denote the absence of a spouse. A marriage is a relationship that exists whether or not a ring is worn, and devotion to Santa Muerte is a relationship that exists whether or not an altar is present. In other words, one does not technically need an altar to successfully petition the Santa Muerte, but if one is able to build an altar, then the altar should be constructed out of respect for the Santa Muerte. Likewise, a wedding ring is not technically required to enter into a marriage, but if you're able to afford a wedding ring, then there is no reason not to invest in one.

The nice thing about Santa Muerte devotion is that there is no doctrine which dictates what an altar should be or how one should be constructed. Many devotees believe that any depiction or representation of death can serve as the foundation for an altar to Santa Muerte. Large, life sized statues of Santa Muerte have been used as altar centerpieces, but so have simple prayer cards that fit in purses and wallets. A cell phone displaying a downloaded image of the Santa Muerte can form the basis for an altar, and so can a rosary or necklace that features a Santa Muerte medallion.

Keeping in mind that the Santa Muerte is the personification of death itself, an altar does not need to depict the Santa Muerte exactly, and any representation of death can serve as an altar to the folk saint. For example, an altar can be established around a plastic skull from a prop shop, or even around a drawing of a skull sketched onto a piece of paper.

For covert devotion, an altar may consist of a collection of symbols associated with Santa Muerte, like globes of Earth (to represent her power over us all), the owl (which represents her wisdom and knowledge of magick), the scales of justice (which represent death as the great equalizer), and the scythe or sickle (which represents the power of Santa Muerte to cut the thread of life). Animal bones and dead houseplants can also serve as centerpieces of altars to Holy Death, because they also represent the energy of death itself.

In addition to the types of altars described already, I have also spoken on my website about the "altar in one's heart". If the only item that is necessary to erect an altar to Santa Muerte is a representation of death, then it is fair to consider here the creation of an astral altar - an altar that exists only in the mind's eye of the devotee. If you're able to visualize a depiction of death in your mind's eye, then consider it a depiction as valid and powerful as any physical depiction.

When you stand before a physical altar, or meditate on a depiction of death in your mind's eye, you make it clear through these actions that you acknowledge the power of Santa Muerte in your life, and that you are approaching the Santa Muerte to make a formal petition - but if no physical altar is possible, and if visualization is not your strong suit, then you can create a type of altar substitute which I will call an altar of declared intent. To be clear, this should only be considered an altar of last resort. To create an altar of declared intent, simply recite one time aloud or to yourself a declarative statement like;

"Santa Muerte, I acknowledge you,
I love you, and now I do petition you,"

Then perform the rest of your petition ritual as normal.

The Magick

If you are able to erect an altar to Santa Muerte, then do so before initiating any sort of magick petition ritual to Santa Muerte, including before initiating the prayer magick described in this book. If it's absolutely impossible to erect any sort of physical altar, or even to conjure an image of an altar in your mind's eye, then don't worry - the magick of Santa Muerte comes from your relationship with death and the intent in your heart, and as a last resort you can speak or pray into existence an altar of declared intent as I described in the previous chapter. The physical altar is a sign of respect which is nice to have, but not required - like the wedding ring described earlier. Only you will know in your own heart whether you are limited by your circumstances or limited by your laziness. If limited by your circumstances, then you have no choice but to roll with the punches. If limited by your laziness, then do not expect anything more than lazy results.

So far we have discussed how the power of Santa Muerte magick comes from our relationship with the folk saint, and that the common denominator of all magick systems is intent. For devotees of Santa Muerte, this means that the more clearly we can express our intent to Santa Muerte, the more likely we will be to have her deliver on our petitions. With the petitions I share on my website, this is accomplished through the use of overlapping symbol representations - herbs that symbolize an intent, oils that symbolize the same intent, colored candles that symbolize the same intent, et cetera. Since this is a book for people who don't have access to the physical tools of magick, the trick is finding a way to express intent in as simple and strong a way as possible, without the physical tools.

Magick Prayer

Santa Muerte prayer magick is magick which primarily relies on the repetition of prayer in order to petition the Santa Muerte and convey our intent. Instead of compiling magick ingredients, grinding herbs, dressing candles, et cetera, I advise devotees to recite a single magick prayer 100 times a day for seven days - that's a total of 700 prayer recitations. The reason we recite the prayer 100 times over seven days is to display our devotion to Santa Muerte; it is a sign of respect that shows our desires are serious, and not frivolous or fleeting. In the absence of our ability to gather magick supplies or even erect a simple altar, the recitation of a single prayer 100 times over seven days shows to the Santa Muerte and to our subconscious mind that we value our relationship with Santa Muerte, that we are not practicing lazy magick, and that we are serious about the objective for which we pray. The purpose of the seven days is purely symbolic and aligns with the fact that devotees are known to offer "seven day candles" as real world offerings to Santa Muerte. We offer seven days of prayer when we cannot provide a physical candle.

It should be noted that it may not take the full seven days for you to begin noticing the positive effects of your efforts, but even if you get exactly what you want before the full seven days, I would still recommend completing the full seven day cycle. The reason is because this kind of prayer magick is intended to replace the magick performed with physical tools, and if you light a candle to Santa Muerte on her altar for a specific wish, you would not extinguish and throw away the candle halfway if the wish was granted early, you would most likely let the candle burn to completion. Also, completing the full seven day cycle may help to ensure that your efforts are not reversed or taken away. So, if you begin a prayer cycle to send away a bully at work, and your bully is offered a job across town on your third day of prayers, failing to complete the seven day prayer cycle may result in your bully's job offer being revoked, putting you right back where you started. Remember that Santa Muerte devotees are *devotees* for a reason. If you devote yourself to a prayer cycle, then you should make every effort to finish what you start.

The prayer must be specific so as to convey your intent and the objective which you hope to achieve. The more clearly the intent and objective can be conveyed, the easier it is for Santa Muerte to understand exactly why you are petitioning. There is always a right way and a wrong way to ask for what you want, and asking for something unclearly may only serve to deliver muddled results. It's one thing to make a general request for money and find a dollar on the sidewalk, it's a much different thing to make a request for money that meets your financial needs.

Although not required, I like prayers offered to Santa Muerte to be prayers that rhyme, because repetition of prayers that rhyme help shift the mind from a normal waking state to a meditative, trance-like state that is receptive to the raising and releasing of magickal energy.

It doesn't matter where you find the prayer which you want to recite for a prayer cycle - you can use one of the prayers I include in this book, you can use the prayers from the petition rituals I share on my website, or you can even write your own. No matter where you find the prayer, it should reference the Santa Muerte in some way, in order to make it clear for whom the prayer is being recited. The prayer should also clearly align with your intent. So long as these two requirements are met - that the Santa Muerte is mentioned and your intent is clearly stated - then you have a recipe for successful Santa Muerte prayer magick.

As you work through your 100 prayers on each day of a seven day prayer cycle, you may find it difficult to keep track of prayers recited and prayers remaining. To reduce confusion, I recommend holding a strand of 100 beads in your hands as you pray, holding the strand at one end and moving up the strand one bead at a time with each recitation of a prayer. When you reach the last bead, you've completed 100 prayers. The same idea would work if you had a cord of 100 knots. If you have access to a Santa Muerte rosary, you can use the five decades of the rosary to keep track of the prayers. Each decade contains 10 beads, which means you would just need to make two revolutions around the five decades of a rosary to keep track of a full set of 100 prayers.

To keep track of your seven days of prayer, you have a few different options. For each day you complete the 100 prayers, you can add an X to the date on a calendar, add an X to a checklist on your phone, tie a knot in a short length of cord, or drop a penny or stone in a jar near the area where you pray. When you have reached seven Xs, knots, pennies, or stones, then you know you've completed your full seven day commitment.

In the event you miss a day of prayers, or manage to lose count of the prayers you have completed, I would recommend starting all over from the beginning. Remember, this method of Santa Muerte prayer magick is not intended for the lazy, it is intended for those who want to petition the Santa Muerte and convey their intent without the use of any physical tools. While we all have a relationship with Santa Muerte, it is our individual effort that will go the farthest in strengthening each of our relationships. If we are serious about our devotion to Santa Muerte, then we should be serious about the commitments we make to her - not because we fear punishment or reprisal, but because it is simply the right thing to do.

Targeting Prayers

One of the characteristics of the Santa Muerte petitions I share on my website is the targeting of those petitions to specific people. For example, if you visit my website, you may notice that many petitions incorporate things like hair or nail clippings, photos, and / or pieces of paper containing personal details, like names and dates of birth. Sometimes a petition may even call for the target's name to be etched into a candle before the candle is set aflame. I refer to these personalized items as target links. Including these types of target links in a magick petition is a method of focusing our intent and making our intent as clear as possible to the Santa Muerte who will hear our petition.

If you happen to be the target of your own petition, a target link is not required, because it would be implied by the use of the first person in your prayer - words like "I", "me", and "mine". If you feel that it would lend power to your petition, however, then there is nothing wrong with including a target link for yourself as the target.

Whether you are targeting yourself or another person, you have a few options for incorporating a target link into your prayer magick. For starters, you can create a prayer that incorporates the name of your target. Another option is to recite a selected prayer while holding or praying over a target link. Locks of hair and nail clippings are still very powerful target links that would work in this instance, but other items that would work may include a photo, business card, or simple piece of paper with the target's name, date of birth, or any other personal details you might know, like address or phone number. If you're using a cord of 100 knots or beads to keep track of your prayers, you could even tie the end of the cord around the target link, then recite the required 100 prayers from the furthest to the closest knot / bead, literally closing in on your target as you pray.

No Guarantees

While it is true that powerful magick can be performed by petitioning the Santa Muerte with crystal clear intent, it is also true that there is only one guarantee in life, and that is our eventual death, not successful magick. Devotees of Santa Muerte do not command the Santa Muerte, for nobody can command death itself - we petition her.

Making a petition to Santa Muerte is not about expecting guaranteed results, it's about increasing our odds of success. When a child asks a parent for a new toy, they generally understand that the parent might refuse; but the child will ask anyway, because the child, on some level, understands that asking is the best way to increase the odds that they will get what they want. Likewise, when a sick person agrees to a medical procedure, they generally understand that the procedure might fail; but they agree because they understand that attempting the procedure may be the best way to increase their odds of survival. This idea is not unique to Santa Muerte magick - it exists across all magickal traditions. Sometimes parents refuse the requests of their children, sometimes the best and brightest doctors fail to help their patients, and sometimes the Santa Muerte does not provide everything that we ask for.

It's nothing against you, it's just a fact of life. If you can understand that, then you will never be disappointed by your efforts to petition the Santa Muerte.

The Prayers

As promised, here are a few prayers which you can use to exercise Santa Muerte prayer magick. Remember, you can also use the prayers from the petitions featured on my website, SantaMuerteMagick.com, or you can write your own.

Prayers for Money

Job Hunter's Magick Prayer

My Saint Death, to you I pray,

For a job with handsome pay.

Overfill my cup for me,

With a job that I can keep.

Clients Come Calling Magick Prayer

Holy Death, Santa Muerte,

Send me clients that can pay.

Let my phone ring off the hook,

With clients ready to book.

Buyers Come Shopping Magick Prayer

Holy Death, I do implore,

Send me buyers to my store.

Let them love the things I sell,

Let them speak of my store well.

Money Lender's Magick Prayer

My Saint Death in cloak of gold,

Please return my money owed.

With your power, close this debt,

Bless me so I may collect.

Prayers for Love

Find a Lover Magick Prayer

My patron Saint Death I pray,

For a lover sent my way.

Send me one who loves me too,

A new love happy and true.

NSA Sex Magick Prayer

Santa Muerte dressed in red,

With hot sex, let me be blessed.

Safe and fun for all involved,

With no strings attached at all.

Prayer for the Home

<u>Peaceful Home Magick Prayer</u>

Home of mine, be blessed I pray,

Filled with peace both night and day.

Holy Death who loves us all,

Keep me / us safe within these walls.

Prayers for Travel

Safe Travel by Land

As I travel tracks and roads,

Holy Death, do keep me close.

Hurt and harm, be kept away,

Safe and sound, both night and day.

.

Safe Travel by Air

Santa Muerte, patron saint,

In the air do keep me safe.

Magick power by your hand,

Keep me safe until I land.

Safe Travel by Sea

As I travel waters blue,

I do keep my faith in you.

On this voyage, I am blessed,

With your magick, Holy Death.

Safe Family Trip Magick Prayer

On this trip which we now take,

Santa Muerte, keep us safe.

May we all return as one,

When this trip is safely done.

Prayers for Help with the Law

Law Keep Away Magick Prayer

Santa Muerte, hear this plea,

Keep the cops away from me.

Send them off when they come near,

Of the law, let me not fear.

Good Luck in Court Magick Prayer

Santa Muerte please support,

The good name of mine in court.

Let the facts be true and fair,

Send a verdict I can bear.

Guilty Person's Court Protection Prayer

Holy Death, mistakes I've made,

Please have mercy with my fate.

When my day of judgment comes,

Bless me with a good outcome.

Prayers for Intuition

Psychic Dreams Magick Prayer

Santa Muerte, show to me,

Psychic visions in my dreams.

As I lay in bed to sleep,

Fill my head with future scenes.

.

Tarot Mastery Magick Prayer

Santa Muerte, oh so wise,

With the cards, open my eyes.

Show me what the future holds,

Through the magick of tarot.

Prayers for Artists

Artist's Muse Magick Prayer

Santa Muerte, send to me,

A muse to set my mind free.

Guide my hand, and effort well,

To make art that I can sell._

Writer's Block Magick Prayer

Holy Death, a writer's friend,

break the block that locks me in.

Give me power to create,

Work that readers will find great.

Prayers for Students

Study Focus Magick Prayer

Holy Death, focus my mind,

To use well, my study time.

Help me so I understand,

My school lessons now at hand.

Good Grades Magick Prayer

As a student, now I pray,

Please bless me, Santa Muerte.

Help me in my quest to learn,

So that good grades I can earn.

Prayers for Healing

Past Trauma Healing Prayer

Trauma which has come and gone,

From you now, I do move on.

With the power of Saint Death,

Demons old are put to rest.

Heal My Body Magick Prayer

My Saint Death, please cast a spell,

Over me to make me well.

In your name sickness be gone,

With your magick I am strong.

Heal Another Magick Prayer

Santa Muerte, heal for me,

This person who has gone weak.

Return to them, strength and health,

Make their body, now be well.

Anti-Addiction Magick Prayer

Santa Muerte, break me free,

From addiction haunting me.

With the power of your grace,

Kill this demon that I face.

Prayers for the Dead and Dying

Dreams of the Departed Magick Prayer

My Saint Death, my Holy Queen,

Lift the veil and bring me dreams,

Of the ones which I have lost,

Gone from Earth, but always loved.

Haunted Home Clearing Magick Prayer

Ghosts who haunt this home of mine,

Leave this place, it is now time.

Holy Death, see them away,

Let only the living stay.

Comfortable Passing Magick Prayer

Body of my loved one weak,

Holy Death I do beseech,

As they pass and cross over,

Please do not let them suffer.

Prayers for Curse

and Hex Protection

Bad Luck Cure Magick Prayer

All this bad luck that's around,

By Holy Death now be bound.

Luck that's good, I now invite,

To flow strong into my life.

Return to Sender Magick Prayer

Holy Death all dressed in black,

Reflect off me all attacks.

Any evil sent my way,

Send it back from where it came.

Prayers for Curse
and Hex Sending

Marriage Destroyed Magick Prayer

What now is one, make it two,

Make their love be done and through.

Santa Muerte, Holy Death,

End this love, put it to rest.

Fitness Goals Destroyed Magick Prayer

Santa Muerte, send this curse,

That my enemy feels worse.

Please destroy their fitness goals,

On their body, take a toll.

Go Away Magick Prayer

Holy Death, I do now pray,

That you do please send away,

This person causing me strife,

This person ruining my life.

Made in the USA
Las Vegas, NV
17 December 2023